LASHONDA WOFFORD
Foreword by Tamara Mitchell-Davis

PAIN EQUALS PURPOSE
I SUFFERED. I LEARNED. I GREW.

Studio Griffin
A Publishing Company
www.studiogriffin.net

Pain Equals Purpose: I Suffered. I Learned. I Grew. Copyright © 2020 Lashonda Wofford

All Rights Reserved. Printed in the United States of America.

No part of this book may be used or reproduced in any manner whatsoever without written permission except in the case of brief quotations embodied in critical articles and reviews.

For information, contact:
Studio Griffin
A Publishing Company
Garner, North Carolina
studiogriffin@outlook.com
www.studiogriffin.net

Cover Design by Ruth E. Griffin
Image by © Lashonda Wofford

Scripture quotations marked NKJV taken from New King James Version Second Edition. Copyright © 1995, 2006 by Thomas Nelson, Inc.

First Edition

ISBN-13: 978-1-7361765-0-4

Library of Congress Control Number: 2020922748

1 2 3 4 5 6 7 8 9 10

I dedicate this book to my late husband, David Akins. You showed me firsthand what true love is. You gave me the precious gift of motherhood. I thank you for sharing your life with us. I will never be able to repay you for all that you gave to me. Thank you for allowing us to experience your life with you. Your life was not in vain. You taught me how to have compassion and what it means to have a heart that desires to care for others, in ways that many people will never understand.

This book is also dedicated to everyone who was a victim of childhood sexual abuse and molestation; to the mothers; and to the victims of violent crimes. I want you all to know that there is a purpose for your pain. Keep fighting and don't give up.

Yes, our stories are full of broken pieces, terrible choices, and ugly truths. But they're also filled with major comebacks, peace in our souls, and grace that saved our lives. Make peace with your stories and walk in your truth unapologetically.

My silence caused someone else to be hurt. It caused someone else to suffer in silence.

Being silent is no longer an option for me. I must share my story, all my story, because now I know and understand that this is not about me. This is so much bigger than I could ever be!

Somebody's breakthrough and healing is tied to my obedience. Somebody's life is depending on my story.

Somebody is ready to give up and my story will help pull them out.

#tellyourstory
#itsnotaboutme
#thisisbiggerthanme
#nomoresilence

Mrs. Lashonda Wofford

TABLE OF CONTENTS

Foreword	1
Introduction	5
Chapter 1: When Life Was Simple	7
Chapter 2: In The Eye Of The Storm	13
Chapter 3: I Was Not Ready	21
Chapter 4: When God Throws A Lifeline	25
Chapter 5: Blindsided	35
Chapter 6: My Emotions Got The Best Of Me	45
Chapter 7: Young, Dumb And Naïve	51
Chapter 8: My Baby Paid The Price	65
Chapter 9: I Just Wanted to Die	69
Chapter 10: God Would Not Let me Die	73
Chapter 11: Why Me?	77
Other Projects by Author	81
Acknowledgements	83
About The Author	85

PAIN EQUALS PURPOSE
I SUFFERED. I LEARNED. I GREW.

FOREWORD

When asked to prepare a foreword for Lashonda's book project, I was honored and gladly accepted the opportunity to do so. You see, when faced with tragedy, obstacles and pain, our main focus is how do we get out of it, how do we overcome, how do we get past it, and what can we do to stop the pain immediately? I mean who really wants to experience pain to begin with? Better yet, who intentionally brings pain upon themselves? My response to that question is NO ONE. Granted, I am speaking from my own experience, but I do believe I would find a few thousand women who would agree with me on that part. NO ONE wants to be in pain: emotionally, mentally, physically, financially, or spiritually.

During childbirth, we want the pain to be over quickly. During surgery, we want the pain to subside. When experiencing heartache attributed from relation-ships or life in general, we want the pain to end. We rarely think about the outcome. We rarely consider the other side of it.

According to Merriam-Webster's online dictionary, pain is "a localized or generalized unpleasant bodily sensation or complex of sensations that causes mild to severe physical discomfort and emotional distress and typically results from bodily disorder (such as injury or disease)." Pain is the result of something.

On the other hand, according to the same online dictionary, purpose is, "something set up as an object or end to be attained: intention." I can't help but wonder how different the pain would be and feel if we placed more focus on the outcome, the intention, the purpose to be found and discovered, rather than focusing on the pain that happened as a result of something else.

I am sure we have all heard this saying before: everything happens for a reason. Whether that is true or not is not up for debate. The point I am hoping to make is that our perspective matters. Our mindset matters. Our ability to change our approach matters. We cannot change people and some things are out of our control, but what we can change is within our own power.

This is why Lashonda's truth is so necessary right now. Here we are during a pandemic, a state of emergency and uncertainty and Lashonda chooses to inspire and bring hope to the lives of others through her own story which resulted from the pain she experienced in her life. It wasn't an easy road. It wasn't a straight and narrow path. There were some peaks and valleys, highs, and lows but through it all she never gave up hope and she never lost her zeal for God. She was determined to keep fighting through her pain in order to land in her purpose, even when she didn't have a clear picture of what that even looked like for her and her daughter.

As we all reflect on life's journey thus far, I am pretty sure we can look back and identify situations that caused pain, some difficult times when we didn't know if we were coming or going or even if we would be able to make it out or make a comeback from it. If you are reading this now, that's proof that you have made it. If you are breathing, that's proof that you still have another chance to get it right, make it right, and even get clear on what you desire for your now and your next. Know that not everything will come easy but make up in your mind that you are determined and hopeful that what's to come is greater than what has already passed.

Lashonda encourages us to seek out purpose even though we may be experiencing pain. To keep pushing forward. To keep God first. To follow our hopes, dreams, and to never give up. Open your mind, pull up a seat, grab your pen, take note, and get ready to receive as Lashonda takes you on the journey of how she found purpose through her pain. Pain that could have prevented her from being where she is today. Pain from choices made that were outside of her control. Pain that found her because she didn't go looking for it. Not only is she writing how it impacted and affected her tremendously, but she is a living and walking example of what it means to be and remain steadfast. All things are possible!

I pray her story moves you closer to God, pushes you into action, and shifts your perspective so that you can experience more abundance than ever before.

> *When you pass through the waters, I will be with you; And through the rivers, they shall not overflow you. When you walk through the fire, you shall not be burned, Nor shall the flame scorch you. Isaiah 43:2 (NKJV)*

Tamara Mitchell-Davis, CEO

TM Davis Enterprise LLC
Author | Speaker | Influencer
Facebook: theceowife
IG: theceowife860
Web: www.theceowife.com

INTRODUCTION

We are all expected to adjust to life but, how do you adjust when you have never been taught about life? How do you adjust to life without warning?

We all experience life in different ways; however, pain is something we've all had to face at some point in our lives. Pain is a result of a traumatic experience that life has thrown at us. The traumatic experiences come without warning; and unfortunately, can happen to us at any point in our lives.

In this book, I will share some of the most traumatic things I've endured throughout my life. These experiences left me broken, hurt, angry and feeling guilty, unworthy, and ashamed. My desire to live had been snatched away from me. I was confused and could not understand how things had gotten to that point. "WHY ME?' I kept asking. I didn't understand at all. I could not escape the pain; and at times, it seemed so unbearable. I was searching for the answers to what seemed to be a million and one questions.

My journey, my process, and my road to healing were not easy and it didn't happen overnight. Yes, there was much pain and many obstacles I had to overcome; however, there was also a beautiful transformation. I know now that God had to break me in order to make me into the woman He desired and required me to be. Follow me on my journey to see how God showed me my purpose through my pain.

CHAPTER 1
When Life Was Simple

Some people spend their entire lives trying to figure out their purpose. This is true even for the people who actually care about what their purpose in life is. I'll admit, I did not think about it until I was older. It is almost like I never had time to think about it as I was too busy trying to navigate through adulting. I often wondered what life would have been like if things had turned out differently but then I must face the fact that my past is what molded me into the woman I am today.

Growing up, people would oftentimes say that my sister and I lived a very sheltered life. I didn't understand why they felt that way until life really happened to me. Then I instantly understood what that actually meant. We had, in fact, lived a sheltered life, one that I am grateful and very appreciative for. My parents worked very hard and always made sure we had everything we needed and wanted. My sister and I were fortunate to be raised by our biological parents in a very loving and nurturing home. As I got older, I realized that we were also spoiled which made me really understand and appreciate our parents even more because of the many sacrifices they made and all the long work weeks they worked just to provide the best life for us.

Life in my eyes was perfect, but I would soon find myself dealing with the harsh reality that most people live every day: that the world can be very cold, and life can be very brutal and harsh.

Let us fast forward to when I was twelve years old—that was when I met my soulmate, David Akins. David and I hit it off from the very beginning and we became best friends. We had a connection that other people could not understand. The world defined him as a thug, but he had this sweet, gentle side to him that very few people ever saw. He had so much heart. He was smart, funny, loving, and brave. David had an unexplainable swagger about him that made you want to get to know him.

He had a twin sister, Hodgie, who my sister and I would often hang out with; and the four of us would have so much fun together. We would walk to school, with David acting as our protector. He made sure everyone knew that they better not even look at us wrong. The older teenagers did not like him at all because he could not be 'punked' by them. As we walked home from school, four out of the five days, he would have to fight a different guy. And every time he won a fight, the older guys would find someone they thought was tougher than he was to beat him. This went on for half the school year before they gave up and gave him the respect that was due to him.

When I was fourteen, my dad accepted a new job at the University of North Carolina at Chapel Hill and our family relocated from Durham to Chapel Hill to make the commute easier on him. David and I had been dating for a while at that point and even though we weren't that far away from each other, moving away meant we could not see each other every day and this felt like the end of the world for us. David promised that we would still be girlfriend and boyfriend even though we were now miles apart. He did not have a house phone, but I remember from the age of fourteen to sixteen, David called me from a pay phone every night and we would talk for hours. He would have to keep feeding the pay phone quarters so that we could continue talking. Rain, sunshine, snow, sleet, winter, spring, summer and fall—I could count on him calling every night. I would tell him he did not have to because I knew what it took for him to call but he did not dare let a day go by without us talking. There were many nights I feared for his life. Being out on the dangerous Durham streets at night was not safe, but he insisted on calling every night and that was it. I hadn't met anyone like David before and it was interesting getting to really know him. He had dreams of owning his own business one day and he wanted to be able to give back to the youth in his neighborhood. We discussed feeding the homeless, providing school supplies and clothing to the youth as well as providing financial support to single moms. He under-stood the struggles single moms faced and really wanted to make a difference for others.

When I was fifteen, my parents agreed to let my sister and I spend the weekend at David's house. We were supposed to be hanging out with Hodgie, but David had other plans. I remember that day like it was yesterday. Later that night, David snuck into his sister's room where we (the girls) were sleeping. He woke me up and whispered in my ear, "Come with me back to my room." He grabbed my hand and led me down the hallway. David had apparently gotten some tips from his older brothers because, when I entered his room, there were candles all around, soft music playing, and his room was actually clean. Although we were very close, we had never gone as far as we were about to go. That Saturday night, I lost my virginity and got pregnant. Yes, we were young, but it was a beautiful experience with my best friend. We were on cloud nine. We were both more in love than we were before.

The following Monday, as we were on our nightly call, David said, "You are pregnant."

There were no signs of pregnancy, so I denied it. Besides, it had only been a few days earlier that we had sex. Still he insisted.

"I know you are, but I want you to know that I love you and I am going to take care of you and my baby."

A few weeks later, my momma looked at me and out the blue, she said, "You are just as pregnant as you can be."

I still showed no signs of being pregnant, so I denied it. But my momma made me an appointment with the doctor to get a pregnancy test done and sure enough, the test came back positive. I was scared to death, and for a while, I was sad because I knew I hurt my momma to her core. Even though my daddy did not say much, I knew he was disappointed in me too. I felt as though they were upset with me because I was so young. I had my whole life ahead of me and more importantly, I had betrayed their trust. I knew that if they really understood the dynamics of my relationship with David, things would have been very different. They would have never agreed to let us visit so freely, let alone sleep over.

Later that night, I told David when he called that I had been to the doctor and I was pregnant. He was so excited. I could not understand why he was not terrified like I was. He told me that he would get to prove to me that he was not going to be a deadbeat like his dad, and he was going to be the best dad he could be.

Even with his support, I was ashamed and scared to go around other family members out of fear of what they might say. I did not want anyone blaming our parents for the choices that we decided to make.

One day, my aunt Geraldine looked at me and said, "This better be the last time I see you hanging around here with your head down. You ain't done no more than nobody else. You ain't the first and you damn sure won't be the last young girl to get pregnant. It's life and it's a blessing. I don't care how old you is." She said, "Boot (my momma) and George (my daddy) are disappointed, but they will come around. Don't you let nobody make you feel less than just because you made a mistake. Everything you wanted to do, you can still do, so stop that crying and moping. Ain't nothing you can do about it now."

This changed the way I looked at my pregnancy and I felt like I could make it.

When I turned sixteen, I got my driver's license; and we were happy because this meant that I could drive to Durham to see David. I saw him every weekend. We were so in love. We grew together and watched each other blossom into young adults.

Lashonda Wofford

CHAPTER 2
In The Eye Of The Storm

David grew up in a single parent home with four other siblings, which made it difficult for him to get a lot of the things he desired. His mother did the best she could with what she had for her children, but she just could not afford the things that other kids had. I watched her for years catch the city bus to and from work to provide food, shelter, and clothes—the necessities.

David fell victim to the streets at an early age. In his eyes, he was a man and he felt that he needed to provide for himself all the things his mother could not afford to get for him—the Jordan's, the Nautica, the Polo, the gold chains, etc. One day, as we were outside playing around, we saw his mother walking from the bus stop carrying bags of groceries after a long day of work. We ran up the street to help her, but even in that moment, I did not know how that affected David. Weeks went by before he told me that watching his mother struggle made him mad. He said, "I've got to do something. My momma deserves so much more. I do not want her riding the city bus, I want her to have a car. I am just tired of watching her struggle to take care of us while he (referring to his dad) is living it up with his new family."

As time went on, I could see the change in his physical appearance and the lifestyle change. He started buying gifts for me and even though he never came out and told me (and I never asked), I knew he had become a drug dealer. It did not change my love for him, but it made me question our lives together. And it made me fearful for his life. Despite that, we promised each other that no matter what we would always be together and have each other's back.

Then on January 29, 1996, I gave birth to our beautiful baby girl. I went into labor a week before my due date. My momma, sister and I had spent the weekend in Goldsboro with our family and on the way back home we decided to stop by Crabtree Valley Mall. We shopped and had a good time. While we were shopping, I started to feel some slight discomfort and cramping in my lower belly, but I thought nothing of it. I wasn't alarmed by this because the image and idea of labor in my head was much worse than what I was feeling. Looking back at it now, I know it was just that my young mind had not processed what was happening to my body at the time. My momma freaked out, but I was calm because I knew my daddy would be waiting on us at the hospital. During my entire pregnancy, I told myself that I would have to stay calm when I went into labor because I knew my momma could not and would not. Being calm in emergency situations was not my momma's strong point. I knew for us to get through it, I would have to stay calm. Besides, she was in control of the car, so I needed her to get us to the hospital safely. My momma, my daddy and my sister were right by my side the whole time. David, however, was at a friend's house watching the Super Bowl and missed the birth; but before the night was over, he was there. He apologized to me a million times and stayed at the hospital with me. That night, we made a promise that we would always love our daughter, protect her, and give her the best life possible.

David was so in love with Babygirl, as he called her. When he first saw her, he cried and as he was holding her, he said to her, "Babygirl, I love you so much and I will always be here for you no matter what." He would just stare at her and smile. He was so proud. He would not let anyone hold her, not even me. He was so excited to change her for the first time even though he was terrified because he didn't want to be too rough and hurt her. I loved to watch him interact with her. Every time she saw him, her face and eyes lit up. He showed up from day one and was a great father.

I was equally in love with her from the first moment I saw her. She was so beautiful to me and everything about her was just so perfect. I could not believe that this little person grew inside me for nine months. Even though we were young, we knew we could not let her down. The world viewed us much different than they viewed older parents. I overheard my momma crying one night, telling my daddy that they had to raise us and now my baby too. They never knew that I heard them, but I used that as motivation not to fail and disappoint them even more. I did not want them to be obligated to care for her but have the option to help us if they wanted to.

When I found out that I was pregnant, I made up in my mind then that I was forever a mother. I wouldn't ever have the option to decide I didn't want to be a mother, even if David decided that he was not ready or simply didn't want to be in her life. I was a mother until I took my last breath and that shaped what I did from there. I went to school during the day and then went to work after school. My parents and my sister were vital parts of my support system, and I know I could not have made it through this without them. Yes, I was sixteen when I gave birth, but she brought more joy to our household. My parents worked different shifts, so they were able to keep her while I went to school, and in the evening my sister helped while I was at work. David would come visit us or we would drive to see him every weekend. He was very intelligent, both academic and street-wise. Even though I graduated from high school and he did not (by choice), he was very smart. He would help me with my schoolwork most of the times. Math problems that I had to write out and use a calculator for he could calculate and solve in his head. I was always blown away by the level of intelligence he had. And because of that, he would read to Babygirl. We subscribed to parenting magazines so that we could get advice and tips on how to be good parents, but experience was the best teacher.

David, however, felt like he was missing out on parts of her life by not living with us, so we decided it was time for us to live together as a family. We were seventeen when we moved in together. Things were going great. He was a loving father and boyfriend and so good to us. He would often tell me that I did not have to work, all he wanted me to do was take care of his Babygirl. I always kept a job though. At one point I had two jobs, but he really did not like that at all. I just did not want to fail or depend on my parents to pay our bills. But David turned out to be a great provider, even despite what people thought. They judged him based on his appearance (nappy hair, baggy jeans, Timberlands and Jordan's) instead of getting to know him.

Pain Equals Purpose

As I stated before, David became a product of the streets at a young age. It took me years to figure out that he was a big-time drug dealer. He was "The Man." Eventually I asked him, "Are you selling drugs?" And he was honest with me—he said yes. However, he refused to give me details or to involve us in that part of his life. He only promised never to bring it to our home or put our lives in danger.

As bad as I wanted to turn the other cheek, I could not continue to act as if I did not see the large stacks of money under our bed or in our closet. Our lifestyle had changed drastically. Every day was like Christmas or a birthday celebration. In his off-time, David would come home with bags of gifts that he bought for Babygirl. She had the best of the best.

In spite of all that, I tried so hard to turn him into a man that made an honest living for life, but my attempts always failed. I convinced him to apply for a job at the company that I was employed with at the time and he agreed to give it an honest try. He applied and got the job and even though he complained everyday he stuck in there. After a month of honest hard work, it was finally payday and that was the end of that. His exact words to me were, "Baby, I know this ain't what people work so hard for. I worked for two weeks and all I got is $500, I can make this in one hour. I'm done with that job." He never went back.

I would bring up the job from time-to-time, but he would not even entertain it. I continued to work as I always did, and a few years went by. We were still doing great, still in love. But in the back of my mind, I was worried about him because of the lifestyle. I didn't pressure him too much because I didn't want to be the cause of an argument. I had gotten use to the routine: from the first to the sixth of the month and then again from the fifteenth to the eighteen he would be gone. I didn't like this part of his life, but I loved him. I just chopped it up to be part of the life style for the woman of a drug dealer. He always paid our rent six to eight months at a time, so I didn't have to worry about that. And even though we always had nothing less than $50,000 in cash in the house, we were not flashy people, so no one ever knew.

I had found a rent-to-own three-bedroom, two-bath home in Cameron, North Carolina and immediately fell in love with it. After looking at it, David asked me, "Do you really want it?" I said yes. I had already thought of a game plan of how to pay the down payment, but he turned to the owner and said, "We will be back to sign paperwork and bring cash tomorrow. Can I leave $1,000 with you today to remove the sign and let people know it is under contract?"

Of course, the owner agreed. We went back the next day and David paid the down payment and six months in advance. We got utilities and cable turned on; and bought new furniture for our house. We were so excited; we were twenty-years-old and already on our way to owning our first home.

David came home one day, after being gone to catch the first of the month money wave, and told me that he needed to talk to me. My heart dropped and my mind instantly started to wonder the absolute worst.

He sat me down and asked, "I need you to be honest. Are you happy with me?"

I was taken back by this question. Where was this conversation going? But I was honest.

"I'm not happy with this lifestyle. We're building a life together, but your name can't go on anything. I love you because you are a good person with a good heart. You are a wonderful father and a great provider, but I am scared to death every time you leave this house because I don't know if you will be back. If something happens to you, what are me and Babygirl supposed to do? Everybody knows that this will only lead you down one of two roads, in prison or dead, and I do not want either. I am always going to be here for you, but one day you need to choose us."

I needed him to understand that all the money meant absolutely nothing if it meant his life or his freedom was on the line.

He then asked me to marry him, but I was not willing to marry him until he gave the lifestyle up.

He admitted he was afraid of coming home one day and we would be gone, but I assured him I would never leave him. We were never in harm's way, and besides that I could never take his daughter away from him.

"This is the only thing I know," he explained to me, "And it's hard, but I'll work on it."

I continued to pray for him daily, that God keep him covered and that David would have a change of heart one day and join the workforce. A few months went by and one day he called me with excitement in his voice.

"Guess what?" he said.

"What?"

"This old head offered me a job!"

"That's great! What will you be doing?"

"It's a moving company so I will be driving the truck, packing people's house up and moving them. Baby, he's going to pay me $1,000 a week cash. I accepted the job and I start Monday."

I was on cloud nine. We celebrated the rest of that week and the weekend. Now I was totally happy. He started the new job in May 2001, and he was so pleased with it.

In August of 2002, we got married. The wedding was beautiful: my uncle married us in my parents' front yard, with our families and close friends there. It was a great day.

CHAPTER 3
I Was Not Ready

On December 20, 2002, our lives changed. David and I had planned to go to the dealership to buy me a Jeep Cherokee. Babygirl and I were Christmas shopping and visiting with my mother in Chatham County, North Carolina. That morning, David had given our daughter gifts that I thought were supposed to be for Christmas considering it was five days away. He wanted her to have them rather than wait. After he was done showering her with them, we got dressed to go meet my mom. I remember he was just staring at us; and I could not and still cannot explain the look he had on his face. He told us he loved us, and he would see us later. We had a long driveway and I remember looking in my rear-view mirror and seeing him just standing in the door watching us drive away. Something was different this time, but I could not figure out what.

I backed up and asked him, "What's wrong? Are you okay?"

He said, "Yes, I'm fine. I just love y'all so much."

I headed down the driveway again, but I will never forget the way he stood in the door watching us go until he could not see the car anymore.

When we got to my parent's house, Babygirl and I got in the car with my momma. We went out shopping to get last minute Christmas gifts for the family. We stopped at my momma's favorite store, Belk and spent a few hours there. Then we went to Family Dollar so that I could buy a box of Christmas cards. As we were waiting in line, my head started hurting bad. I got lightheaded and felt like I was going to pass out. I tried to shake it off and ignore it, but it got so intense, I felt like I had been hit in the head. I told my momma that I was ready to go, but she laughed and joked, "I know you are not ready to stop shopping. No, not you."

Once she realized I was serious, and my head really was hurting, we quickly checked out and went back to their house. She gave me some Tylenol for my head. After about forty-five minutes, the pain eased up, so I proceeded to write out my Christmas cards. As I was writing out my last one, the phone rang. It was an unknown number. At the time, if someone were calling from unknown or private numbers, they would have to state their name. I answered the phone and listened as the caller said their name. It was David's mother. When I heard her voice, I instantly knew something was wrong, I just did not know what exactly. She proceeded to tell me that David had been shot and she was not sure if he was dead or alive.

I do not remember the rest of the conversation, but I do recall my mother taking the phone from me. We then rushed to the emergency room (ER) at Duke Hospital. The hour drive suddenly felt like hours. My momma, of course, called my daddy, who was a security guard at Duke. I asked her to ask him to check on David and tell me if he was okay. He couldn't get to him, but I could tell by my daddy's tone that he knew it was bad. I remember walking in and his mom giving me a hug and as she hugged me, she said, "I am so sorry…" Then I was instantly being bombarded by doctors asking a million and one questions.

When I finally got to see David, I felt like the wind had been knocked out of me. I did not recognize him from the swelling and all the tubes protruding out of him. His features were so altered, I just could not believe my eyes. All I could smell was blood and medication. There were twenty plus machines, with at least twenty bags of intravenous (IV) medications. The sound of the ventilator and the pulse ox machine, used to measure the heart rate and oxygen level, is a sound I will never forget. My world was shattered. I could not think and the pain that radiated through my body straight to my heart was unbearable. I literally just could not catch my breath.

The doctors explained to me that David had been shot five times in his right arm, his left thigh, his right side, his head, and the back of his neck. The bullet to the back of his neck had actually cut his spinal cord in half. He was unable to breathe on his own, was paralyzed from the neck down, had severe swelling and bleeding on the brain; and he went without oxygen for more than fifteen minutes. He was found in a pool of blood, unresponsive hours after he had been shot. Paramedics had revived him on the scene, but he was in a coma now and they could not tell me if he would or wouldn't wake up.

"I'm sorry, sweetheart, but he will not live through the night," the doctor told me.

I remember wondering why would someone do this to him and then just leave him there to die? I could not believe any of this. I felt like I was having an out-of-body experience. It just did not seem real. All I could do was cry and when I thought about our six-year-old daughter, my heart broke all over again for her. How was I going to explain this to her? As I looked at David just lying there helpless, I felt hopeless. I wanted him to move or something to give me just a little bit of hope, but nothing happened.

I remember joining the other families in the Intensive Care Unit (ICU) waiting room that night and every time I heard a code, I held my breath thinking it was David. I did not sleep at all and I never left the hospital. The next morning, he was still alive, but the prognosis looked very bad. Doctors called a meeting with the family and again went over everything that was wrong and not functioning properly. This time they gave him another twenty-four hours to live. They started asking me about donating his organs and taking him off life support. I did not want to hear any of that. No one was getting any of his organs and I was not removing life support.

After the next twenty-four-hour period was up, the doctors called another meeting to inform us again that if he lived, his quality of life would be poor. They assured me that he would never walk or talk again, he would always have a tracheostomy (a medical procedure that involves creating an opening in the neck in order to place a tube into a person's windpipe, below the vocal cords, to allow air to enter the lungs; breathing is then done through the tube, bypassing the mouth, nose and throat) and a ventilator; and his cognitive abilities would be little-to-none. They had no hope for him.

CHAPTER 4
When God Throws A Lifeline

At this point, I was sick and tired of these meetings with all the negative talk, continually telling us what wasn't and what wouldn't be, so I asked them to develop a plan past twenty-four hours and give me everything they had on ventilator-dependent quadriplegics. It felt like something went off inside me, like an internal switch was turned on. David was not giving up and neither was I. I began to pray harder than I ever prayed in my entire life. I sought God for guidance and understanding, but most of all, to accept whatever His will was.

I stayed in the waiting room, day-in and day-out, reading up on his condition because I could not help him and advocate for him if I knew nothing about his situation. He couldn't talk so I had to be his voice. He had no use of his limbs, so I had to move for him. He couldn't think for himself, so I had to think for him. David and I had promised each other that if something ever happened to either of us, the other person would care for the one who was ill. I told him if something happened to me and he could not take care of me to take me back to my momma and daddy and vice-versa. We did not like facilities; I worked in a nursing home at the time and I did not like what I saw. This wasn't something I would ever do for anyone that I loved.

Normally, hospitals don't allow young children in ICU, but because everything was touch and go with David, they allowed our daughter to visit him. The first time she saw him, she was just so happy, she sat on a bar stool that I brought from home so that she would be tall enough to see him; and she talked and talked to him. She told him she had to catch him up and proceeded to do that. It was so sweet to watch her and every time she visited, she would just talk to him as if she did not see the tracheostomy, the ventilator and all those other tubes. All she saw was her daddy. Then before we left, she would kiss him and say, "I love you, daddy, and I will see you later."

After the shooting, David was in a coma for about one month. During that time, we would go in and talk to him. I would sing to him. Babygirl and I recorded a song, and us talking to him and that recording would play when no one was there in his room to talk to him. When he woke up, he didn't remember anything. What came next was one of the hardest things I ever had to do: I had to explain to him what happened, tell him that he was paralyzed from the neck down and that he couldn't breathe on his own. The tracheostomy (or trach), ventilator, feeding tube, suprapubic catheter (a device inserted into the bladder to drain urine out if someone can't urinate on their own), pulse ox, and all the medications were now permanent and vital parts of his life. He was so upset, he cried for days. He was processing everything that we had been dealing with. I felt so bad for him, but what could we do?

As time went on, he started remembering what happened to him; and for me, honestly, it was better when he couldn't so he wouldn't know that someone shot him five times and left him there to die. Facing that reality was a very hard pill to swallow.

One day, as I was reading about the complications of individuals who are bed-ridden or bed-bound, I came across an article about pressure sores or pressure ulcers. It stated that if the individual wasn't turned and repositioned every two hours, they could develop these. The article decried them as being horrible and hard to handle if they were not prevented or caught in time. They were classified into Stages 1-4 with 4 being the worst. I realized while reading this article that I had never seen any of the nurses turn or reposition him, so I asked them if he had any pressure areas.

"Yes, he has a small area on his back side," a nurse told me.

I decided I wanted to see it, so I stayed in the room that day while they did his bath. When they turned him over, his oxygen level dropped, and I nearly passed out. The small area was nowhere near small. According to the article, this was already a Stage 4. It had a very foul odor, and I could put my whole hand in it.

I was furious at this point, and felt like we had been betrayed and lied to by doctors and staff. I caused a big scene. This was totally unacceptable. I could not understand how someone could develop something that was preventable and serious in the ICU Unit of what was believed to be one of the best hospitals. In all the round table discussions, no one mentioned the sores at all. I felt horrible, like I had already failed him. This happened on my watch. I knew I had to do something very different if he was going to have any type of fighting chance.

After weeks of having a pity party, I was able to snap back and regroup so that I could make rational decisions, ones that would be in the best interest of David, decisions that were not made based on pure emotions. I felt like I was in a whirlwind with limited time to prepare. I had so many thoughts going through my head and so many emotions, the biggest one being fear. I was so scared, and I started second guessing myself in every decision.

Later that night, as I sat in the waiting room, I began to cry uncontrollably, just nonstop like never before. I felt like my heart had been ripped out, and my lungs could not get enough air no matter what I did. I began to pray, and I specially remembered asking God, "WHY?" I needed Him to show me the way, to strengthen me but most of all, to help me understand what we were to take away from all of this. I asked God to give me a sign or something to let me know if he would make it, and if I had made the right decisions this far.

In the mist of my breakdown, I did not realize that someone else had entered the waiting room. Her name was Beth, and she was an older lady who was there because her sister was fighting for her life in ICU as well. She looked at me with tears in her eyes and said, 'Baby, God don't make no mistakes and even though I know you're in a bad place right now and you are not sure if your husband will pull through, just continue to do what you are doing. Hold your position and trust that GOD is with you even in what seems to be the fight of your life." She gave me a big hug and said, "I admire you for being willing to step up and fight for your husband's life because he can't. Most women your age would have never stayed to deal with none of this and to be honest I probably would not either."

From that night forward, Beth and I bonded, and I didn't spend any more nights alone in the waiting room. She had a hotel room near the hospital but every night I stayed in the waiting room, she stayed with me. She bought a big air mattress with covers and we would sleep on that at night until the waiting room was full again. I could feel myself getting mentally stronger, day-by-day.

Some of the families that were in there when David was shot had left, their loved ones having gone home, to rehab, or died. New families were being added every day. I developed some really good relationships with those families and even though I was the youngest wife there, they had the same respect for me as I had for them. I would have never thought in a million years that something like this would happen to us, but I could see God moving, slowly but surely.

On January 29, 2003, our Babygirl turned seven-years-old but of course her dad was still fighting for his life in ICU. We could not celebrate like we normally would, but it was still special. My parents brought her to the hospital. David's immediate family was there as well as a few friends we met while on this journey. We had cake and celebrated her birthday. People we knew and people we did not know bought gifts for her because by now, everyone knew our story and knew who we were. David's older sister went to the hospital gift shop and bought Babygirl a stuffed animal (a yellow lion) as a gift from her dad and she was so happy. She cherished that lion, taking him everywhere she went and sleeping with it every night.

Looking at her, I realized I had a lot to be thankful for and a lot to fight for. The bond that she shared with her dad was so beautiful to me, it motivated me to make sure she had her dad around as long as possible. My mom, dad and sister were definitely my rocks. I leaned on them the most, especially to help look after Babygirl while I spent all my time at the hospital with her dad. They made sure she got to school, ate, bathed and everything. I would see them on the weekends when they came to sit with me at the hospital for support.

David's mom and siblings were also there but as time went on, they had to get back to work. Even then, they would still make time to come to the hospital to visit with him and check on me. Days, weeks, and months went by and the emotional ride never ended. One day things would look good, the next day new infections would arise, and his condition went back to serious and unstable. It got to the point where ICU visiting hours really did not apply to me anymore. The staff allowed me to spend as much time with David as I wanted. I had begun to get incredibly involved (hands on) with his care and I was able to get comfortable with things. If I weren't there, he would give the nurses attitude and not follow certain commands until they called me back to the room.

Even though David was paralyzed from the neck down and on a ventilator, cognitively he was all there. His brain simply needed time to heal. He and I developed a stronger bond than ever before. We came up with a simple way that he could communicate 'yes' or 'no' answers—he would blink twice for yes and once for no. Simple right? When he was in a bad mood though, he would not do either and this was why the nurses would just allow me to stay after visiting hours were over.

One night, David was having a really hard time. He had been in that hospital bed for months with nothing but time to think about and process everything that happened to him. I had been in the waiting room taking a mental break while his older brother was visiting with him. After the visit was over, I went back into the room and David looked so sad. I asked if he was okay and he didn't blink which meant he was giving me attitude. I stopped talking, pulled my chair up next to the bed, laid my head on his legs and went to sleep. I woke up and he was sleeping so I went back to sleep. It was quiet for hours but around 3 am he woke up, looking for me as I had moved my chair back into the corner. This was where I sat when I was visibly upset so that he couldn't see me cry. That night, I was very emotional about everything that was going on and trying to figure things out. I pulled my chair back next to the bed so that he could see that I was still there and as I did that I noticed tears rolling down his face. For the first time in months, he was crying and noticeably distraught. I began to ask questions, trying to figure out what was wrong. The first question I asked was a hard one, but I had to ask.

"Do you want to continue to live this way?"

He blinked his eyes twice, which meant yes.

"Will you let me know if you change your mind and decide it's too much?"

He answered yes.

"Do you want to see Babygirl?"

He answered yes.

"Do you miss her?"

He answered yes.

I told him that I would arrange to have his mother bring her the next day. He just stared at me while he cried.

"Does it have something to do with me?"

He answered yes.

"Are you worried about me?"

He answered yes.

I told him not to worry about me and not to worry about me leaving him because I would never do that to him or our child.

He was so upset they had to give him something for anxiety. He finally went to sleep and slept most of the next day too. Up until this point, it never occurred to me to reassure him that I wasn't going to leave him. I just assumed he knew, which was kind of foolish on my part. I was so busy making sure he was getting the proper care, I hadn't even considered anything else.

Fast forward to March 2003, doctors began to meet with the family to discuss placement options for him because at this point they had done all that they could do for him. They had gotten him stable enough to be transported. After the first meeting, I made the decision to have him transferred to our home so I could care for him. My heart would not allow me to place him in any type of facility.

Two weeks went by and doctors scheduled a follow-up meeting to begin the paperwork for placement into a skilled facility better known as a nursing home. In the meeting, I informed the doctors and his family of my decision to care for him at home. I explained to them that at twenty-two-years old he had no business living in a nursing home. He had a healthy wife, mother and four abled-body siblings—we could all care for him together with help from private duty nursing.

Of course, everyone tried to talk me out of it. The doctors said it was too much to care for someone in his condition. His mother cried and begged me not to take him home.

"It is going to require a lot from you, and you are so young, sweetheart. You have your whole life ahead of you," she told me.

I could not understand how she could be so willing to just throw him away as if his life didn't matter.

Even with all of this though, I still decided he was coming home. I knew I was young, and I knew it was going to require a lot of sacrifices on my part, but I was up for the challenge. Bringing him home would also mean that he could get one-on-one good, quality care; and that he could spend as much time with our daughter as he wanted. He could watch her and be a part of her life. They could continue building the bond that they shared, and I could keep my family together as long as possible. This was what bringing him home meant to me. I explained all that to the family and I thought they would understand but they did not.

Lashonda Wofford

CHAPTER 5
Blindsided

Minutes before we were scheduled to meet with doctors again to show them our plan on how we would care for David at home, his mother told me, "We have decided that it's just best if he doesn't go home." She made this decision with her children, leaving me out of it. I was devastated, but my decision was final. We went into the meeting with the doctors and I explained to them that I needed more time because his family decided they could not help. I needed to lean on my family now. Caring for a loved one at home was not new to us because I watched my mother and aunts care for my grandmother at home. They all pulled together, and everyone had specific shifts and duties. Granted, my grandmother and David's conditions weren't even remotely the same but, they both required around the clock care.

I called my mother after the meeting, crying my eyes out. She could not understand anything I was saying at first, but after a while, I was finally able to get the words out. She and my dad came and spent the rest of the day at the hospital with me. I was able to regroup and refocus. I must admit I felt betrayed and blindsided by his family, but I did not have time to ponder over that. I called my uncle who was an ER nurse at the time and explained the situation to him. Together, we formulated a plan and a schedule. God is so good, and this is an example of how

I knew He was working on our behalf even though at times it did not feel like it. I had been approved to receive twenty hours of skilled nursing care for David, 24-hours a day, 7-days a week, 365-days a year. This meant that I would only have to cover four hours each day. I would care for him the four hours and my uncle would come down on his weekends off to help. I presented this plan to the doctors and it was approved; they started the process to get him transported home with everything he needed. I looked at his family differently from that point on, but they made the decision that was best for them and I made the decision that was best for my family.

Now looking back, I understand that most people cannot get out of themselves long enough to have to always put someone else's needs before yours, and caring for David did seem very intimidating. They were right, it was a very difficult task, but how can we say, "It can't be done," if we never try? How could we be too afraid to even try?

The next two months were extremely critical as I was put to the test plenty of times by the nurses and doctors. I had to prove that I could care for David properly before he could go home. I had to learn how to suction him properly. Individuals who require a tracheostomy no longer have the ability to cough mucus up, so suctioning is required multiple times throughout the day and night to help keep their lungs free of that build up. I had to learn how to do tube feedings and how to clean his trach and his gastrostomy tube (g-tube), a tube which had been placed through the skin of David's abdomen straight to his stomach to help provide nutrition since he could no longer swallow solid foods. I had to learn how to troubleshoot when something went wrong with any of the equipment, how to bag him if his o2 sats (blood oxygen levels) dropped low. Most importantly, I had to learn the ventilator and every detail about it. I had a hard time at first because I scared myself. I knew this was his lifeline and anything that went wrong wouldn't be good. His life was literally in my hands and I did not want to fail him, our daughter, or his family. I was locked in his hospital room with a respiratory therapist who was very firm with me. She made me learn that ventilator in just a few hours. Inside and out. She would make it go off and I had to troubleshoot things and figure it out on my own. I could not have asked for a better teacher. She was very hard on me, but she believed I could do it just as much as I did and that is why she was so hard on me. Even though I was under a lot of pressure, I had to get it all done right if I wanted to take my husband home. The doctors thought I was crazy and of course they advised me differently, but they couldn't deny my request.

After months of intense training and preparing, we were three weeks away from our discharge date. My mother picked me up from the hospital one day and we went shopping at Walmart. I had to buy everything we needed to prepare David's room and get everything set up. We basically had to turn one room in our house into a mini-ICU room. We had money saved up and I was relieved about that because I did not have to worry about how I was going to pay for it all.

We stayed in the hospital from December 2002 until June 2003, but we were finally ready to take David home. He was so excited, and the family was too. The day that we had been waiting on was finally here…discharge day.

I remember feeling so many different emotions then. Excitement, confusion, nervousness, and lots of fear. As you can imagine, fear took over because even though he was being discharged, David's condition was far from being permanently stable. I prayed so much and so hard during this ordeal but the human emotions at times tried to get the best of me. Yet, every time, God would remind me that He was in control and had equipped me with all I needed to carry this assignment out. Whenever my emotions would start getting the best of me, an overwhelming sense of peace and calmness would come over me and once again things were crystal clear. I would look up and say, "Thank you, again, Lord."

Discharge day was here, and we took the hour and a half ride from Durham to Cameron. The long ambulance ride really took a toll on everyone but there was no time to rest. Once we finally arrived home and I got David settled, he took a long, well-needed nap. Now keep in mind we were supposed to have 24-hour skilled nursing care for the first thirty days, then twenty hours moving forward seven days per week. This was when I discovered the home health agency that accepted our case and were contracted to provide the care did not have sufficient or trained nurses for our case. This meant I would end up covering all the hours, from Thursday morning at 7am until 7pm Monday evenings. This went on for about one year. The agency only provided coverage Monday night from 7pm until 7am Thursday morning. I had to develop a schedule for the days I had to care for David on my own.

7am   Wash his face and brush his teeth.

8am	Meds and feedings via feeding pump and sometimes bowels.
9am	Watch TV or he would sleep.
11am	Mid-morning medications and breathing treatments.
12pm	Bathing and grooming time.

Bath time would take anywhere between two to three hours depending on how things went. If David needed to be shaved, I would shave him first, then cut his hair if it needed to be cut. Then we could prepare a good bed bath with lots of soap and water. I never knew how long this process would take because things would happen in the middle of the bath and that became the priority. For example, during bath time his colostomy bag or suprapubic catheter might leak. This meant I would have to stop with the bath, change the colostomy site and bag, change the suprapubic catheter, then proceed with the bath. Because his condition was touch and go, every time I turned him on his side or towards his back side to change his sheets, his o2 sats would drop. When this happened, I would have to bag him or manually give him breaths through his trach and suction him continuously to bring them back up. This could take anywhere from fifteen to forty-five minutes. After that was done, I would continue with his bath. At that point, the water was cold so I would have to get more hot water to continue. Once his bath was completed, it was time to clean the trach and G-tube sites.

4pm	Time for meds, breathing treatments, suction, and tube feedings. Sometimes,

	David would sleep for a couple of hours because this took a lot out of him.
6pm	More meds. David would watch TV or spend time with Babygirl.
7pm	Phone call with his mom. She would always call and talk with him from 7pm-7:20pm.
7:20pm	Watch TV and nap or talk to the nurse until 9pm. Nurse Dorris would read to him, watch TV with him and just tell him about her kids etc. She was really good with him and took excellent care of him. They had a bond.

On the nights that I had coverage for him, I would go to bed around 9 or 10pm. If I didn't have coverage, then I would set alarms through the night to give him his meds. I had a baby monitor set up so that I could hear him if he needed me. But really, the baby monitor was on whether I had coverage or not.

I know this sounds like an easy task and it probably would have been if he were on a ventilator, but then the o2 sats would drop, and his blood pressure would bottom out every time I turned him halfway on his side. I remember the first day this happened. I was alone without a nurse, so I had to figure it out. I almost panicked but when I looked into his eyes, I could see fear and I had to reassure him that I was not going to fail him, and that everything was going to be just fine. I closed my eyes, took a deep breath and that overwhelming sense of peace and calmness came over me; and step-by-step I was able to provide him with manual breaths and increased his o2 to bring things back within normal ranges for him. He looked at me, smiled and then began crying. He was thankful and from that point on he had confidence in me. He knew then I could care for him.

After two hours, the bath was done. Then it was time to shave him and some days, cut his hair. This was something I had to learn how to do, and over time I became better and better. This entire process initially took four hours but, as time went on, I learned how to do it all in about two and a half hours. He would sleep well after this, waking up in enough time to talk with our daughter once she got off the bus. She would come straight in from school every day and go into his room to tell him all about her day. She would get in bed with him and watch TV and talk. Every time I saw them together, it made all my work worth it. I was reminded that this was not about me.

At 5pm, it was time for more meds. Then again at 7pm, 10pm and 11pm. Sometimes he would need to be suctioned or get breathing treatments throughout the night; and if he were on IV antibiotics, those would have to be given throughout the night as well, only for everything to start all over again at 7am.

David's condition was so fragile in the beginning that I had to make a pallet on the floor next to his bed so that if the vent went off, or he needed suctioning through the night, I would be right there. He could not breathe for a second without that ventilator so I could not take any chances. My worst fear was having to call his mother and tell her he was no longer with us. This went on for a year until I found another agency to provide the service. This company came in and it was like a breath of fresh air. They had nurses available to cover all 20-hours, 7-days per week. They covered 7am-4pm then 7pm-7am so that I was only responsible for covering 4pm-7pm. I had gotten accustomed to not sleeping all night, let alone in my bed, and the first night I finally did get to sleep, I felt like a new person.

After having consistent coverage, I decided to go back to school to become a BSN, RN (Registered Nurse with a bachelor's degree). But then, I had a change in staff and the new daytime nurse wasn't reliable as the previous nurse, so I stopped attending school. I attempted to complete nursing school a few times before I just became totally frustrated with the whole thing. I chopped it up as another thing I would not get to do.

As time went on, I realized that my passion for respiratory therapy outweighed my passion for nursing. Caring for David forced me to learn the in's-and-out's about trach's, ventilators, breathing treatments, etc. I learned that being a nurse and being a respiratory therapist were two different jobs with different scopes of practice. I realized that there were so many things that we (people with the full use of all limbs) took for granted, like breathing on our own, scratching our own head, and just being able to reposition ourselves whenever we wanted to. I realized I could do this for the rest of my life and be totally fine.

David's unique situation also afforded me the opportunity to witness firsthand how the general population treated the ventilator-dependent quadriplegic community. Initially, I was taken aback by some of the remarks that most medical professionals would use when referring to someone in David's condition or someone they viewed as less valuable because of their disability.

Pain Equals Purpose

Often the comments were, "He don't know what's going on," or "It doesn't matter, he can't feel anything anyway." They would talk about him in front of him and or standing over his bed. The level of disrespect from them was also unbelievable. Many times, I let them know up front that certain behaviors, conversations, looks, opinions, and negativity wouldn't be tolerated and that his brain was intact, so he was able to comprehend everything that was going on.

I would always accompany him and the nurses to all doctor appointments, and hospital visits. David was prone to pneumonia more than most people because of the ventilator so we would often have to make short visits to the ER for blood work, x-rays and to start IV therapy. It was certainly a fact that admitting him to the hospital to receive IV therapy would always result in him picking up other harmful things. While in the hospital, I talked with the primary care physician and together we decided that he would never be admitted for treatments that he could receive at home. The fact that he received 20-hours of skilled nursing care, 7-days per week on top of me being well-trained and competent to care for him weighed heavily on the primary care physician approving my request.

Lashonda Wofford

CHAPTER 6
My Emotions Got The Best Of Me

I remember one day seeing the mailperson delivering mail and attempting to put mail into our mailbox. When she couldn't fit it in, she came to the door. I answered it.

"Hey sweetie, are your parents home?" she asked.

I did not even feel like explaining that I was the adult, so I just simply replied, "No, ma'am."

She gave me all the mail and said, "I'm sorry to bother you, but it was full."

This made me so sad and I became emotional after realizing I had not been outside in over a month. I felt like I did not have a life outside of being a full-time caregiver for my husband and a full-time mother to our child.

But then, my sadness turned into anger because I felt as though everyone else was living their life the way that they wanted to, but I couldn't. All those people who used to call on him for money and everything else were nowhere to be found. I felt alone. I could not wrap my brain around the fact that his mother could just continue living her life as though David was not lying in a hospital bed, totally helpless and unable to move at all. I could not understand why she would not even try to care for him. How could she just move on with her life as if none of this was going on? There was not a day that went by that she would not call to check on him and then ask to talk to him. Granted, he could not talk back because of the tracheostomy, but he could hear her voice and understand what was being said to him. His face would light up every time she called, and he would tell me to tell her that he loved her. I knew she loved him, but my question was how she could not try to care for him. How was she sleeping at night? His brothers and sisters did not even try either. They never helped and barely came to visit.

During my emotional breakdown, I heard a voice that said to me, "Remember you made the decision that was best for you. You wanted to keep your family together. You chose to put their needs before yours. Everything is going to be fine and it's okay to get tired but giving up is not an option. I need you to remember that this is not about you."

It was God, speaking to me. He continued: "Have you ever considered the fact that it is hard for his mother to watch her baby lying in bed day after day, totally dependent on you and strangers? That this is something that his mother cannot physically do? That she needs time to process her own feelings to figure out how to move forward in life now that this has happened? If your heart was shattered into a million pieces when this happened, how do you think she felt? His siblings are not obligated to care for him even though he is their little brother. His family's life had just begun, and they were trying to figure out their own life. You are his wife, and you accepted the challenges of being a full-time caregiver to your husband and a full-time mother to your child. You are not alone; I am right here. I need you to trust Me, focus on your family, and continue to pray."

WOW! My pity party was over.

Pain Equals Purpose

In that moment, I realized that it was not my place to question everyone else's decisions. God did it again. He gave me new strength and the desire to pray for David's family. That day, I began to pray for them; I prayed for peace, understanding and healing. I prayed that one day their hearts would allow them to see him as a person when they looked at him instead of the crime that had put him in that bed. I prayed for his mother throughout the day because when I really sat down to think about things from her prospective, I knew I couldn't walk a day in her shoes. As a mother, I could not imagine having to go through what she had gone through with David and cope with the harsh reality that he was now faced with.

This is how I know that prayer changes things because suddenly, his family became a little bit more involved. His oldest brother would call before but now he was calling and coming to visit with him. David was so happy. He began to look forward to his brother's visits. As time went on, his oldest brother grew more and more comfortable with David and his condition. He would make the three-hour drive to spend the day with us. This allowed me to go to the grocery store, pick up meds, wash clothes and spend time with our daughter. David's older brother became very involved in our daughter's life. When he called, he now checked on her as well as David. He also started attending school programs.

I told God, "Okay, I see You moving."

As time went on, his mother started visiting on a regular basis. The days she could spend the night were huge for all of us. David was so happy and, most importantly, my daughter was starting to see that they had not forgotten about her. They spent time with her on their visits as well. I remember David's mom coming down to visit and she would cook, clean, wash clothes and so much more. I didn't always feel like cooking a full course meal so when she cooked us a good home cooked meal (and she can cook), it was a treat.

One day, she said to me, "If you have some errands to run or something, you can go ahead. I'm here."

This made my heart beam because that meant she was now comfortable enough to stay at home with David alone.

I asked her, "Are you sure?"

She looked at me with her big, beautiful smile and said, "Yes, I am sure."

I told her I would make sure David didn't need to be suctioned or anything else before I left, then I ran my errands. I went to the grocery store and to the pharmacy to pick up more medications for David. I was gone for about thirty minutes. When I came back, he was sleeping, and his mom was sitting right next to his bed reading a book. They were so peaceful.

Now that we were finally settled in at home, it was time to go to trial. The District Attorney had officially charged the man who shot David. Going to trial was awful. It felt like just as I was able to pull it together and figure out how to move forward I had to relive this nightmare all over again. The trial was actually a lot worse than living it. You hear details you had never heard before and not all the details were good. I remember sitting in the court room thinking, WHY would this man do this to him? What kind of animal treated people this way? The man responsible for shooting David had a criminal record that was twenty pages long. I could not help but wonder why he was not already in prison.

The trial lasted for years and the man wasn't sentenced until after David died. I remember his attorney was doing her closing arguments as she tried to convince the jury that he should get a lighter sentence because he had a young daughter who was only three or four years old at the time. This made me so angry. I couldn't believe that she was really trying to use this as a way to reduce his sentence. When it was my turn to give my statement, I said, "The fact that they're trying to reduce his sentence because of his young daughter is just disgusting to me. I don't give a flying flip if she never gets to see her dad again because if these are the kinds of lessons and examples, he's going to teach her, she is better off without him in her life. Everyone is trying to get sympathy for him and his daughter but who considered the fact that my baby will never see her dad again? When she wants to see him and talk to him, I have to drive her to the grave yard. I don't care about him or his daughter. He should be put away for life like the animal he is."

Now that I'm older, I regret saying the things I said the way I said them. I could have expressed them in a much nicer way. I can't help but wonder how mean that must have sounded to his daughter being that she was so young, But I was hurt and I was angry because I felt like they didn't care about my daughter's wellbeing as she would have to now grow up without her father. I felt like they didn't value David's life because of the lifestyle he chose to live. It didn't make him any less human than anyone else. I felt like they were not even trying to make sure justice was served. This was when I learned that the judicial system was not designed for the victims but for the criminals. He was sentenced to eleven years in prison for murder.

CHAPTER 7
Young, Dumb And Naive

When the new agency stepped in, things were so much better. I finally had reliable nurses that were just what we needed. I had one nurse, Ronnie, who would always go above and beyond the call of duty. I was so grateful to him for helping me out. At first, I was hesitant to accept all this extra help because I didn't know what his angle was, but, as time went on, my guard came down and I trusted him way more than I should have. Then, I found myself in a web of a mess that felt like I would never get out of: I became involved in a sexual relationship with this man. I'm not sure how this happened. I think the combination of my loneliness and feeling desirable may have played a major role in my actions at the time. I felt so convicted but, for whatever reason, I continued this relationship.

After six months, I found out he was married with kids. Talk about feeling convicted. I tried breaking it off because it was wrong. Even though David couldn't take care of my physical and emotional needs, he was still my husband. I loved him and I never wanted to hurt him. But not just that: now there was a wife and kids who could be affected by this affair. I never wanted to be the woman who causes another woman pain. Yet here I was. This was bad. Ronnie threatened to tell David, the owner of the agency, and to report me to Department of Social

Services (DSS) for neglecting my husband and daughter. He knew that they were the most important things in my life. He also knew that I feared David being placed in a nursing home and my daughter being taken away from me, so he used this to his advantage. I believed that he would turn me in and that everyone would side with him because, after all. I had been having a sexual relationship with this married man and I was married too. No one knew about the threats nor that I was basically being forced to stay in a relationship that I had no desire to be a part of. What I thought was an answered prayer turned out to be the worst nightmare ever.

I would often wonder why a 41-year-old man would want to be sexually involved with a 21-year-old. I asked him one day and he became upset. This was the first red flag. It didn't feel good and I lived with guilt every day. I was in way over my head. It had gotten to the point where I could not stomach his face so I would work all his scheduled shifts and just have him pay me $3,000 every two weeks to do his job. He never had to show up for his scheduled shifts. This solved my money issues, but my problems were far from over. Our families were intertwined—his kids and my daughter became best of friends, and strangely, his wife and I became close. She told me that they were only together for the kids and that he was not the person she fell in love with and married: he had changed over the years. All of this had my mind going constantly. I felt so bad because I knew she was still in love with him and she was hopeful that the person she married would show back up one day, but I also knew he was living a double life, far from the person she thought he was. Now looking back, I realized there were many lines that were crossed, and rules overlooked professionally, personally, and morally.

Prior to Ronnie being assigned to our case, I prayed and asked God to provide a way for me to be able to continue to afford to pay all the bills, to financially continue to be able to provide for my family. It didn't take long to see the savings dwindle down to nothing and the only thing I had to depend on was the Supplementary Security Income (SSI) check and the check from DSS. To maintain everything, it took all that and then some. It had gotten to the point that I had no money to take care of my basic needs. I relied on my parents for that. Everything I had coming in went to the bills and to David and Babygirl's needs. At one point, it was so bad, I contemplated moving back home but I didn't know what would happen to David, so I couldn't do that. I prayed and asked for help to be able to financially support my family. I guess in some strange way I thought my prayers had been answered with Ronnie. But I would spend the next few years trying to get away from him.

Getting out of the mess was nowhere as easy as getting into it. David loved Ronnie and Babygirl had also grown very fond of him. I had numerous conversations with him trying to explain to him how I wanted out and how our affair should have never happened. He knew I believed in God, so every time I would bring up the fact that we were both living a life of sin, he would say, "God knew you needed someone, so He sent me."

My response was, "God would never send me someone else's husband. That's not how God works." He would get so angry every time I would say this to him. After a while, he could see that he was losing control of the situation, meaning I didn't care about making him mad. I just wanted out. He threatened to kill me, to kill David and or to tell him about us. It was terrible. After he realized I was enjoying him not coming in to cover his scheduled shifts, he started showing up to work then but he would still pay me. I would lock my room door at night to keep him out and on the weekends Babygirl and I would leave while he stayed there to care for David. I threatened to tell his wife, but he didn't care. He told me she already knew. I would spend hours in my room crying and praying like never before. I made a promise to God and myself that if I made it out of this thing alive, I would never look at, talk to, or touch another woman's man whether it be a boyfriend, 'boo', 'suga' and, definitely not, her husband.

I started saving money so that I could buy my own car because I had to separate myself from him. I didn't have a car at the time, so I needed to drive one of his cars. I was so miserable and I'm not sure when I noticed the shift in his eyes, but they became dark and evil-looking. I honestly think this was because he realized that he was losing control and I was figuring things out. I actually despised him. I did not trust him anymore and I thought he might try to make good on those threats to kill me or hurt David to make it look like I did it. I was so stressed out and my heart was so heavy. I couldn't sleep at night. I couldn't get my mind to stop. I was in way too deep, but I didn't know how to get out.

One day, I noticed David was presenting signs of pneumonia, so I called the doctor. Then I called Ronnie to inform him as well. Of course, he came over to assess David and help me get him prepared for transport to Cape

Pain Equals Purpose

Fear Valley Hospital via Harnett County EMS. Once we got him loaded onto the ambulance, Ronnie left. I decided not to ride with David that day because I needed to drive so that I could make it back home before Babygirl got off the bus. I drove behind the ambulance like I had done a million times before. When we arrived at the hospital though, I noticed David was very still and quiet. Normally he looked around for me, to make sure I was there. This time, however, his eyes and mouth were wide open. I asked the emergency medical technician (EMT) if everything was okay, if anything had happened on the way. But of course they denied anything was wrong. I looked for the heart monitor and pulse ox machine, but neither was present. When we finally got into a room, one of the regular respiratory therapists walked in, took one look at David, and started yelling for the doctor.

"Get the doctor in here now," were her exact words. I knew David was in trouble then.

The ER doctor came running in, looked at me and said, "Ma'am, I'm going to have to ask you to leave."

I looked at him and said, "No! Whatever y'all are getting ready to do, I've already seen or had to do myself."

They quickly hooked him up to the heart monitor and all I saw was a flat line. The doctor turned to me and said, "Ma'am, I am sorry for your loss," and just like that, David was gone. They didn't try to revive him or anything and I'm not sure why they didn't even attempt.

I was in total disbelief. I asked them to leave the monitor on for a few minutes but there was still no heartbeat, just a flat line. I will never forget that sound. I had failed David, my baby, his mom, and his family. I had to make the one call that I never wanted to make: to inform his mother that her baby had passed.

I sat there in that hospital room with him for hours just trying to replay the events in my head. What did I miss? Why didn't the paramedics let me know he was in distress? How did a routine thirty-minute ride result in his death? How was I going to tell my baby that her dad was gone because I wasn't there for him?

So many unanswered questions.

A little bit later, I had a conversation with the doctor who pronounced him dead. I asked him to be honest with me. David was fine when I put him on the back of the ambulance. All his vitals were normal. What happened? Specifically, I had three questions for the doctor:

Did David just die?

Did EMT's report what his vitals were at the time of arrival?

Did EMT's call in to report a change in status prior to them arriving?

The doctor responded with a 'No' each time. He said, "Sweetie, you're right. You are dead on with everything you're asking and I'm sorry, I wish we could have done more. I called to speak to the supervisor and request copies of the run reports from their heart monitor, pulse ox, etc., but I haven't received them."

Once his family came to see and visit with David, I had to go home and tell my baby that her dad was gone. This was one of the hardest things I ever had to do. I knew it was going to break her heart and there was nothing I could do to help her. I also knew she was going to have a lot of questions that I just didn't have the answers to. To be fair, we all were in total disbelief. I couldn't understand how David could have survived getting shot five times, endure multiple surgeries and setbacks, live for six years longer than doctors anticipated, just to lose his life to negligence by four Harnett County EMT's.

The next few days would prove to be some of the hardest; and to be totally honest, I didn't even want to deal with them because every time I thought about the reality of what was going on, I would have to face the fact that I failed David miserably. I didn't even want to get out of bed, but I knew I had to keep pressing. I didn't realize that David's death was out of my control and for some strange reason I thought that I could have saved him if I had just ridden with them; or they would have just pulled over to let me know he was in trouble so I could help. There were so many things going through my head, but I think of all the emotions, guilt weighed the heaviest on me. The guilt of knowing that I had failed him. The guilt of knowing that I had been having an affair with a married man right under our roof. The guilt that I felt for crying to God every night asking Him to please help me because things had gotten way out of hand and I was tired. Guilt that I failed Babygirl and his family. I was supposed to care for David, watch out for him. Respect him no matter what and love him unconditionally and I failed to do that.

I spent years afterward trying to cope with the guilt and shame of the whole situation. I remember my uncle saying to me at one point, "Shon, it's not your fault. If God wanted it to go any other way, it would have. You thought you were in control, but you wasn't. God knew you were tired, and that David was tired so this was His will. You did all you could for so many years and look at how much longer he was here with you and Tada (our daughter)."

To this day, I don't think my uncle knew how much his words actually meant to me. From that day moving forward, every time the shame tried to weigh me down, I could hear my uncle's voice reminding me that it wasn't my fault. Each day after that, things got a little easier.

I also learned to be very intentional and strategic with my prayers and relationship with God. I never understood how powerful the words that you pray in your prayers are and what you petition God for, because you will get it. I know now that when you pray to God for something you must also pray and ask for peace and understanding with whatever God's will is. This was and still is a very vital part of my prayer life. It's so important to be able to accept God's will because it's always better than the plans that we have for our own lives.

Trying to plan David's funeral was also extremely hard because, even though I was the wife, I wanted to allow his family to input what they would like as well. It wasn't easy, though. I was emotionally drained, so I had to lean on my mom a lot to shut down all the foolishness. I wanted him to be buried at the church that I was a member of because it was close to where Babygirl and I lived. His family wanted him to be buried at a cemetery in Durham. I picked out a certain casket and the family thought it was too hard. I was able to be very hands-on with the presentation of David's body for the service. I cut his hair, I shaved him as well because this would be the last time I would ever get to touch, groom, care for and see him here on earth.

Pain Equals Purpose

Outside of family, God strategically placed people around me who stepped in and helped any way they could. The Chatham County Community and the Church that I was a member of showed me so much love, it was unbelievable. My pastor at the time and my church family, were truly amazing, keeping us lifted in prayer, food, monetary donations—real genuine love. Here I was thinking that by living in Harnett County, nobody knew what I was dealing with, but they did. So many people remembered our story because it was the front-page news for months and any time something changed, it made the news again. I will forever be grateful to these angels who helped pull me out.

God wasn't done sending angels, though. The owner of the home health agency that we were with at the time of David's passing offered to cover the cost of the funeral but David's family had an insurance policy on him that paid for everything, and once I told the home health agency owner this, she said, "Well, I'm going to give the money to you and your daughter so that you can provide for y'all until you can get on your feet and get a job." And she did just that. For months, every two weeks, she would leave a check for me at her office for $3,000 to $4,000, totaling well over $10,000. I was humbly grateful.

As I started picking up the pieces of my broken life, I still had this dark cloud hanging over my head—the toxic relationship with Ronnie. One day, I told him I was done, that our affair should have never happened. He didn't believe me, and of course, attempted to make threats to kill me. At that point though, I didn't care. I was no longer scared of him or his threats. I did not speak to him again about ending the affair and I explained to my daughter that we would be looking for a new place to stay but not to tell him. My daughter didn't know about the threats and she didn't know the dynamics of our relationship. It was important to me to make sure she went with me to look at apartments because I wanted to include her in the process of us starting our lives over. I wanted her to know that I valued her opinion, and we were in this together, We would go look in different cities because I wanted to get as far away from Ronnie as I could. I found a very nice apartment tucked away outside the city limits of Sanford but then the plan changed.

One day, Travis, who is my now-husband, called to offer his condolences for David's passing. I told him that I was taking steps towards getting my own place because I was really done with Ronnie and I was no longer going to deal with him. Travis knew about the affair and he also knew about the threats. He offered to let us move in with him and his roommate and said they would protect us from Ronnie.

"That way you won't have to work three jobs, seven days a week. I know your daughter is smart and she understands that you need to work but she really needs to spend time with you because she lost her dad." Travis knew that after David's passing I took a few months to gather myself but then I went to work to help support us. I had three jobs and I worked seven days a week. I went to the office from 9am-12pm; then went to my second job from 12pm-5pm. I had a client that I cared for from 11pm-7am and I did this over and over for about two years.

Mind you, Babygirl had been around Travis, and my family knew him as well, so he wasn't just some random person that we were moving in with. But now I had two plans in play. I finally had enough money saved up for a nice down payment on a car. I went to the Nissan dealership in Sanford and I got approved for a Nissan Altima. I was in love with that car.

The first thing I did was pick my daughter up from school so that she could see that we had our own car now. I then went to work at the home care agency as the Office Manager. All my family, co-workers and bosses were so happy for me. Thirty days went by, but I didn't get any information about how to make payments, so I called my mom and asked her what I should do. She advised me to call the dealership, so I did, and boy did I regret making that call. I was told I had to bring the car back because they couldn't get it financed: I was a 1099 employee instead of a W-2. I was devastated and, in my mind, it was a major setback.

I remember being sad and crying uncontrollably. My boss at the time sat me down and said, "What you whining over that car for? People kill me trying to do what they want to do. Have you ever thought that this is not the car that God wants for you? Take the freaking car back, take your money back and put it on another car."

I drove around for another thirty days before I returned the car. About a week later, I passed a dealership where I saw a black Mazda 6, so I stopped to look at it. However when I got there, I saw a beautiful Burgundy 540I BMW parked next to it. I automatically told myself I couldn't afford that kind of car. A salesman talked to me about the Mazda and I started the application process to get approved for the car. It took longer than I thought it should. I had to go to work, and I didn't want to be late.

So the salesman said he would continue working on the deal and give me a call once it was approved.

At work, I told my client about the Mazda and how I was hoping to get it that day. A few hours later, my cell phone rang and sure enough it was the salesman.

"Lashonda, I just wanted to let you know that everything has been approved and you can come pick up your BMW whenever you're ready."

I burst into tears and asked him to repeat himself three times.

"You were actually approved for both, but I saw your eyes when you looked at that BMW. You can afford it, so it's yours if you still want it," he said.

I thanked him, but mentioned that I wouldn't be able to get it until the next day because I was at work. My client and I cried with joy the rest of my twelve-hour shift. I also called my mom and dad as well as my boss to tell them the good news. I didn't tell my boss what kind of car it was, she was just so happy for me that I had gotten another car; and being an independent contractor wasn't an issue this time. I told her I was going to need a ride the next day on my lunch to go pick my car up.

She said, "Girl, what are you coming in here for? You better go to the dealership first thing in the morning so you can drive yourself here!"

I was on cloud nine, I did not sleep at all that night. I went to the dealership the next morning and the car was parked out front with a 'sold' sign on it. I was in tears. The salesman was genuinely happy for me; he said, "Sweetheart, when I see you, I see my daughter and I'm not sure what you're going through but you deserve this car. Don't ever settle for less. Let's get this paperwork signed and I want you to thank God as you drive away in your new BMW."

I could not believe that this car was mine. I drove and cried because this is what God wanted for me. My mind was seriously blown. As I was driving, I could see all the people looking at me. The car was definitely a head-turner. I went to the office and parked in the back. I walked in and my boss looked out the front door.

"So where is it?"

"I parked in the back."

We went outside.

"I know this ain't the car," she said when she saw it.

"Yes, ma'am, it is," I told her.

She cried and said, "Now do you see what I was trying to tell you? You were trying to hold on to something that God didn't want for you. Lashonda, do you understand if this is what God wants for you at twenty-five-years old, can you imagine where He will take you in a few years?"

We sat in that car and talked. She was so happy for me. She gave me the day off and I went home and parked in the middle of my front yard to wait for Babygirl to come home. She was so excited when she found out we had our own car, and not one we had to take back.

"Mommy, it's so pretty," she said as she rubbed her hands around on the car.

I called my parents, and they were so excited. They told me to drive to them so that they could see it and they would give me gas money.

Later on that night, Travis called to check on us.

"Guess what," I told him, still excited.

"What?"

"I bought a new car today," I exclaimed.

He was happy for me and asked me about it.

"It's a beautiful burgundy 540I BMW," I told him.

"Wow, that's great," he replied and added, "I bought a new car today too."

It was a Pontiac G6 and I was so happy for him. We were super delighted for each other. And now that I had a car, it was time for me to work on getting away from Ronnie. I had to move away. My family didn't know how bad things actually were because I never wanted to worry them or lose my daddy as a result of him killing Ronnie. I also felt like this situation was my pay back for sleeping with a married man so in my mind, I thought, "I made this bed of fire; now I have to get burned by the flames before I can get out."

One day, I just decided that enough was enough and with the help of Travis, we made arrangements to have us moved out of the place I was renting and in with him and his roommate. As we were moving my belongings, Ronnie showed up and, of course, tried to show off by making threats, but at that point, I just wanted to be done with him and this entire so-called relationship. I told him to get out the way because since he refused to leave me alone and stop just showing up at my house, we were moving out and he could have the house all to himself.

He tried calling and harassing, but nothing worked because I was determined to get my life back on track and end this relationship. After the move, things started moving in the right direction.

CHAPTER 8
My Baby Paid The Price

A few months went by and Ronnie finally stopped calling, texting, following me and driving past my place of employment. Our life seemed to be back to normal and happy. I felt like the weight had been lifted from my shoulders and my mind. For the first time in a long time, I could breathe easy. I had become an active member at my church, my prayer life was still on 1000. I could not help but wonder if God had really forgiven me for sleeping with a married man and mistaking this trick of the enemy for a blessing from Him. I was so gullible. Guilt and shame consumed me for many years. In the back of my mind, I was waiting on someone to come along and take my new life away from me. I was sure karma would find me. And it did.

About seven months after we moved out to start over, my daughter's grades started dropping. This was very unusual for her—she was always an A-student. I remember riding her hard day in and day out trying to understand what was causing this. We had arranged to have a mutual childhood friend, who was now a pastor, come and bless the house; to pray over our new home and our lives. As he walked through our house praying with his anointing oil, he kept doubling back to Babygirl's room and each time, he would pray harder and harder.

He was feeling something, but God did not reveal to him what he was feeling.

When he was done blessing the house, he told us to pray for Babygirl because something had her troubled and weighted down.

"She is burdened down and I am not sure why," he said, "But the enemy has no room here. He is already defeated."

As a mother, that crushed me because, at that very moment, I knew my child was unhappy. Something was troubling her, and I didn't know what that was, which meant I didn't know how to help her. I immediately started praying for my child, two, three and sometimes four times a day, asking God to keep her mind and give her peace. My prayer was that if she was not comfortable enough to talk to me that she talk to someone else.

I asked God to reveal to me what was wrong. A few weeks went by before God answered my prayer. I remember getting off work and picking Babygirl up from school. We had a good conversation on our hour ride home, so I was not prepared for what was to come.

Later that evening, I found a letter written to me by Babygirl. And as I read it, my heart shattered into a million pieces. My daughter apologized to me for the way she had been acting, for her grades dropping and for making me cry. She then went on to explain to me how she had been getting molested by the man I had been in a relationship with. This had been happening since she was seven-years-old and now she was thirteen.

My body went numb, and suddenly, I could not read anything else on the paper. It looked like another language. I felt nauseous, and instantly felt pain radiating through my body. One of the things that I was supposed to do as her mother was to protect her and I failed her miserably. As I cried and lost my mind, my daughter came in my room, hugged me, and apologized for not telling me. We hugged and cried together. I explained to her that she did not do anything wrong and that I was not upset with her at all. Still, rage and anger took over.

"I'm going to kill him," I declared and called Travis. He didn't answer though because he was still at work, so I called my parents to tell them and to ask them to come over and watch Babygirl for a little while. I told her that my parents were coming over and that they would be there with her for a little while until I got back.

But she only hugged me and said, "Mommy, don't do it. Daddy is already dead and if you do something to Mr. Ronnie, you're going to prison and then I won't have either of my parents with me. I know that grandma, grandpa, auntie, and Mr. Travis will do what they can to raise me, but I need you."

I called Ronnie and told him that I was going to kill him if he ever came near my daughter again. He tried to deny it all. I also told him that I was going to report him first thing the next morning. I called his wife to talk to her because at this point she needed to take her kids and get as far away from him as possible. When I explained to her what Babygirl had told me, she said that she didn't believe it and that Babygirl was lying.

I was livid and I cursed her out. In my mind, I couldn't understand how she could say that she didn't believe her? What reason did she have to lie? I told her that if she continued to allow other people's kids to come over and stay the night, she was just as much to blame as he was and that she was a fool for not packing her kids up and leaving. I asked her who she thought he would turn to now that he would never be able to harm my child again. Her kids were not off limit, and she was wrong if she didn't get them out of there.

A few weeks went by and my boss at the time asked me how I was doing, and I said I am okay. She asked me if I had spoken with Ronnie's wife and I said no. I am never talking to her again and her response to me was, "Don't you think you are being a little harsh on his wife? She is just as much a victim as you and your daughter. Think about it. His wife is clueless as to the monster he really is. She can't see him as a child molester. He is bringing her to court to show her off, but she is brainwashed. She does nothing without him telling her or giving her permission. All she sees is the person he pretended to be and that is the man she is hoping to get back."

As time went on, I really thought about it and my old boss was right. I guess I was too harsh on her and I didn't have to say all the mean and harsh things I said to her. None of this was her fault and I was wrong for telling her that I was going to kill her and him. I didn't know what else to do and those were my true, raw feelings at the time. I could have told her what happened just so that she knew but then it was up to her to remove her kids and other people's kids from his life. I was just so upset with her because she continued to put her kids and other kids in harm's way. The type of pain that this caused me is something I don't wish on anyone.

CHAPTER 9
I Just Wanted To Die

The next day we went to the local sheriff's department to report everything. I had to admit that I didn't know how I missed all the red flags. I had allowed the abuse to happen.

I cannot explain what the next few years would be like for us because even to this day I cannot describe what I was feeling. I was at my lowest and I did not want to do anything: I did not want to pray, go to church or anything; and for a while I did not do any of it. I was upset with God, because I could not understand why he would allow something like this to happen to my child. I felt like she had already gone through so much in her little life, why did she have to go through this too? I must admit that for the first time in my life I wanted to die. I just wanted to end it all. I wanted to lay down and never wake up. For years, I cried myself to sleep at night. I was obsessed with trying to find ways to ruin their lives.

As I struggled to mend the pieces of my shattered heart and life, one day I had an 'aha' moment. I asked myself, "What part did you play in this? How can you blame God for the decisions you made? You can't blame God because He never told you to sleep with someone else's husband. Nothing about that situation was Godly."

I had to accept that my daughter being sexually abused was my fault and that was not an easy pill to swallow. Every decision I made led us to where we were at that very moment. I lived in so much misery for the next few years. Honestly, I had days where I was down mentally from this. I had to learn to just bite the bullet and face the fact that my wrong doings caused all of this. I felt like David was no longer resting in peace; like I had failed him and her again. I second guessed everything about my life. I was so afraid of the world, and my trust was no longer so easily given.

During this time, God blessed me with a wonderful husband in Travis. He was able to withstand the storms that my karma brought. He was a man and not a boy. Life had beaten me up, but my husband gave me hope. He prayed for me and my daughter when we could not find the words to pray. He stepped up to the plate and held our hands through every courtroom visit and every meeting with the district attorneys. He held me every night as I cried myself to sleep. He spoke life into me when I couldn't see why life was worth living. He reassured my daughter that he would always protect her and no one else would ever hurt her again. He assured me that none of this was my fault and that there was no way I could have known that Ronnie was a serial rapist. My husband literally loved me back to life.

On the day of the hearing, Ronnie and his wife showed up at the courthouse together, holding hands, dressed in matching colors, acting as if they were a perfect couple. That didn't bother me as much as it bothered me to see that his wife was reading the Bible in the courtroom. This made me livid and I wanted to kill them both. I didn't understand how she could be there supporting him after knowing what he had done to my child for years. How could she continue to allow other children to be around him, subjecting them to his evil ways?

Ronnie pled guilty and was sentenced to jail time. He also had to register as a sex offender for a minimum of twenty years. From there, I spent years trying to figure out how to make Ronnie's life a living hell. I went to the sex offender registry, got his picture, and then printed 500 color copies, and posted them all over town. I submitted a copy to the North Carolina Board of Nursing as well. I didn't want him to continue hiding behind his scrubs and taking advantage of people to get close to their kids.

Lashonda Wofford

CHAPTER 10
God Would Not Let Me Die

Watching my daughter struggle to deal with and process everything that happened to her because of me made waking up each day unbearable. But once I was able to accept responsibility for the part I played, to accept God's forgiveness and, most of all, forgive myself, things got a little better. I felt like I could breathe a little easier.

Now that I had gotten myself in a better place, I had to find the courage to apologize to my daughter and ask for her forgiveness. This was harder than everything else. I mean, how do you say to your only child, "I am sorry for putting you in harm's way. I am sorry for sleeping with a married pedophile. You paid dearly for my wrong doings or mistakes. I am sorry that what should have been. Bad karma came full circle back around to me and to you and you had to pay the ultimate price for my mistakes and my bad choices."

How to talk to her was my biggest question but eventually we did. We talked about everything and she did not blame me at all. In fact, she saw us all as victims—her, me, the nurse's wife. When I look at everything from this view, I know she's right. I am so amazed at how mature she has dealt with this entire thing. My daughter is so incredible, and I admire her so much.

After we talked, cried, and hugged each other, I realized that I was blaming myself when she was not.

Parts of me could not help but to feel down about it all. I realized again in that moment just how amazing God was. He allowed my daughter to be strong enough for the both of us when I was not. He allowed me to be strong enough for the both of us when she was not. God never allowed both of us to be down at the same time.

We all have things that we are not proud of and this is that thing for me. Now I know better and I try to tell parents that every decision they make directly affects their child/children whether they believe it or not. I try to get them to make better decisions, so they don't have to worry about the terrible consequences that come with making those bad decisions. Who's the karma going to catch up to from their ill ways?

As much pain as this brought me, I am truly grateful each day because even though the situation was bad, I know that it could have been much worse. I could have lost my mind, went to prison for murder, lost my child in the pain while she was trying to deal with it all or her future could have been dimmed. "BUT GOD," is all I can say. God has allowed my baby to not only graduate from high school, but she has also earned her bachelor's degree in nursing and has a wonderful career as an ER nurse that she loves.

I found my true passion and purpose during all my pain. I am grateful for the life that David and I shared. Through that experience God gave me a vision and this is where my home-care agency Akins Helping Hands was birthed from. Akins Helping Hands assists individuals with their daily living and instrumental activities in the privacy of their homes. Akins Helping Hands gives me the opportunity to serve and pour everything that I learned while I was caring for David into the individuals that we now care for. My experience with David taught me compassion, love, and how to genuinely care for those who can't care for themselves. It gives me the opportunity to advocate and speak out for others. It also allows me to serve and care for others while keeping their dignity intact, respecting them and their families.

Lashonda Wofford

CHAPTER 11
Why Me?

I asked myself, "WHY ME?" so many times. One day, God said to me, "WHY NOT YOU? You have been through hell on earth, but I have always pulled you out. You walked through the fire and yes, you are bruised but you're not burnt. I always made sure you made it through. I know at times it felt like I was not there, but I have never left your side. I had to break you to make you. To shape you and mold you into the person I require you to be.

"Akins Helping Hands will thrive because it is fueled by the passion and love you have for David. You will always operate from that place of compassion. Your pure heart will be a helping hand to others. You will use your compassion and your kind heart to be the voice for others, to help pull them from those dark places you once were in. You will always remember to extend to others the same, love, grace, and mercy that I have given you."

David's life was not in vain; it was important. His life and legacy will be carried out through me and my works. Akins Helping Hands is important to the health care industry. It is a resource for the ventilator dependent quadriplegic community, but it does not stop there. Akins Helping Hands also advocates, supports, and educates other families that find themselves in similar situations.

God is allowing us to serve our community by providing excellent In-Home Care Services.

You will give a voice for survivors of child hood sexual abuse and their families. You will share your testimonies to help someone else start their journey to healing. After reading this book, the things I hope you take away from this are:

1. Always try to find the sunlight in the midst of darkness.
2. Remember, it is not about you.
3. Ask God to show you the lesson and the WHY in the pain.
4. Push past the pain.
5. If God did it for us, He can do it for you.

Through my deepest pain, I have truly found my purpose, I found my WHY. My prayer is that you'll find yours. I pray that my testimonies will help you get your breakthrough and move past those things that have hurt you.

Pain Equals Purpose

Lashonda Wofford

OTHER PROJECTS BY AUTHOR

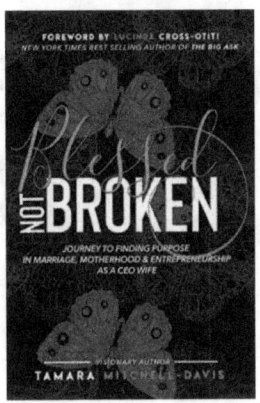

BLESSED NOT BROKEN
**Journey to Finding Purpose in Marriage,
Motherhood & Entrepreneurship as a CEO Wife**

Blessed Not Broken introduces you to ten women who have overcome their broken dreams and circumstances to receive varied, but wonderful blessings and lessons. Each author tells her unique story about dreaming, planning, working, failing, praying, and becoming the CEO of her own business, her family, her purpose-driven life.

In these stories, these women also speak frankly and openly about the challenges of honoring promises made to spouses, to their children, to themselves, and ultimately, to God. Though each woman is distinct, and the particular struggles each faces are different, their shared quest to fulfill God's purpose, and rise to their potential is the inspirational thread that binds them all together.

As you meet these valiant women through the stories they tell, be touched, be motivated, be entertained, be changed… be blessed.

Coming Soon

Pain Equals Purpose: Journal

Pain Equals Purpose: Volume 2

Other Products

Affirmation Collection

Visit https://mailchi.mp/iammrslashondawofford/i-am-mrs-lashonda-wofford to purchase autographed copies of the author's books, and products from the Affirmation Collection; or to get more information.

ACKNOWLEDGEMENTS

First and foremost, I would like to thank God for putting me through the test and allowing me to come out gracefully. For allowing me to share my testimonies to inspire, encourage and motivate others. I would like to thank my husband, Travis Wofford, for being such an amazing husband and father. Thank you for being my rock. I want you to know that your support means everything to me. Thank you for accepting and loving me, flaws, and all. The good, the bad and the ugly truths. Thank you for accepting what my life was prior to you and what David and his life meant to me. I want to thank my beautiful, amazing daughter for always trusting and believing in me. Thank you to the CEO Wife, Tamara Mitchell-Davis, for being my mentor and writing the foreword. Thank you for everything you have taught me about writing and being an author. Thank you to my family and friends for your love and support. Special thanks to my mother, my father, my sister, and my niece for always having my back and pushing me and supporting me. Lastly, thank you to my amazing sister coauthor Catherine Latoya Grant-Alston for taking time out of her busy schedule to assist me with my first solo book project.

Lashonda Wofford

ABOUT THE AUTHOR

My name is Lashonda Renee Wofford. I was born to George and Beverly Williams in Goldsboro, North Carolina. I am happily married to my wonderful husband, Travis Wofford, for eleven years. I am the proud mother of two, one biological daughter, and one son, whom my husband and I have raised since the age of six. I am also a proud grandmother of one grandson, Cam'Ron Jackson-Walker, six years old. My family and I are faithful members of Grace AME Zion Church in Raleigh, North Carolina.

In addition to my family's long-standing church membership, I have actively led the praise and worship team and sang in multiple church choirs. I am currently pursuing a degree as a Registered Respiratory Therapist while running the day to day operations of Akins Helping Hands. Akins Helping Hands is a privately family-owned business that provides in-home care to the elderly and individuals battling illnesses that require hands-on assistance with Activities of Daily Living and Instrumental Activities of Daily Living. The organization is led by myself, as the CEO/Administrator, and my husband as the CEO. Akins Helping Hands has been in business since 2015 and we are still serving our own and surrounding communities today.

I am the Founder of GRACE Community Outreach INC. GRACE is a non-profit organization that helps feed and clothe the less-fortunate, provides support for victims of child sexual abuse and their families, as well as provides support to individuals battling with cancer. Through these organizations, I have been able to really fulfill my purpose in life and I am honored and thankful to God for choosing me for such a task. People often feel like we are helping so many people, but the reality is that serving people in these different capacities has been such a blessing to me and my family. We don't take any of it for granted. I look forward to bigger and better in the years to come!

I am also a Number One Best-Selling Author, International Speaker and the mastermind behind The Affirmation Collection which was launched in July of 2020. Keep an eye out for the next volume of Pain Equals Purpose: Living Out My Purpose.

Pain Equals Purpose

Lashonda Wofford

www.ingramcontent.com/pod-product-compliance
Lightning Source LLC
Chambersburg PA
CBHW070048120526
44589CB00034B/1602